# The *Most* **Dangerous Storms** *on Earth*

by Barbara Keeler
illustrated by Steve Gardner

Harcourt

Orlando   Boston   Dallas   Chicago   San Diego

Visit *The Learning Site!*

**www.harcourtschool.com**

Every year a number of hurricanes sweep across the oceans. Known as typhoons in the South China Sea and cyclones in the Indian Ocean, hurricanes cause more extensive destruction than any other type of storm. Their winds can reach velocities of more than 200 miles (322 km) per hour. These storms can be hundreds of miles wide, last for several days or weeks, and travel hundreds or thousands of miles.

## Horrible Hurricanes

In September of 1998, Hurricane Georges rampaged through the Caribbean. Savage winds with speeds as high as 150 miles (242 km) per hour buffeted island after island, flattening everything in their paths. Flying debris smashed into the structures the winds left standing. Georges dumped as much as 20 inches (50.8 cm) of rain on some islands, swelling rivers, immersing homes, and burying dozens of people under tons of mud.

After ravaging the Caribbean, Hurricane Georges went northwest and slammed into parts of Florida, Alabama, Louisiana, and Mississippi. Its winds demolished some structures, and its torrents of rain washed away or flooded others. Because many residents were evacuated from the areas in the storm's path, people in the United States were able to avoid widespread fatalities and to protect some property. Unfortunately, in the Caribbean, Georges left 400,000 people dead and many more homeless.

## What Causes Storms?

The same causes are at the root of all storms and weather changes: uneven heating of Earth's surface, differences in air pressure, and evaporation and condensation.

**Uneven Heating**  The most fundamental cause of hurricanes and other storms is the uneven heating and cooling of Earth's surface. Earth is heated by solar radiation, which is the energy in the sun's rays. Because of Earth's curved surface, its uneven elevations and differing terrain, and the distribution of water and land masses, its exterior is not heated evenly.

**At any given moment, the sun's rays are striking some parts of Earth directly, at right angles. Other parts of Earth are in shadow or receiving the sun's rays at a slant, or at oblique angles. Temperatures are highest where the sun's rays strike at right angles.**

The sun's rays strike Earth most directly, at right angles, at or near the equator. Moving north and south from the equator, the sun's rays begin to slant down at greater angles. Direct rays heat Earth's surface much more than indirect rays do. Because of the direct angle of the sun's rays, places near the equator receive a disproportionate amount of the sun's energy and are warmer than places farther north or south. Temperatures are coldest at the poles, where the angle of the sun's rays is most oblique.

Different areas in the same region might be heated unevenly as well. For example, solids such as soil and rocks absorb the sun's radiation much faster than water does, and they also release it faster. You may have noticed that on a hot day, dark surfaces, such as black asphalt streets, are hotter than light surfaces, such as cement sidewalks. This is because dark surfaces absorb more of the sun's energy than light surfaces.

Irregular elevations of land can also cause uneven heating. When the sun rises near a mountain, its rays begin to warm the slopes of the mountain long before they beat down on the valley floor.

You might think that Earth's atmosphere is warmed by the sun's energy. In fact, it is the energy absorbed by Earth that heats the atmosphere above it. Very little of the sun's energy is absorbed or retained as it enters the atmosphere. The higher in the atmosphere that air is, the cooler it is. This is because air receives most of its heat from the rocks, soil, and water below.

**Differences in Air Pressure** As energy from Earth heats the air, the warm air rises. You can see the action of warm ascending air if you watch ashes or sparks rise rapidly over a blazing fire.

The pressure of air in Earth's atmosphere pushes against Earth and all objects on it. Warm air ascending creates areas of low pressure, and cold air descending causes high pressure. Air moves from areas of high pressure to areas of low pressure. You can observe this movement if you release air from a tire. The air in a tire has greater pressure than the surrounding atmosphere, and it pushes against the sides of the tire. When an opening is made in a tire or the valve is opened, the air rushes from the tire into the surrounding atmosphere.

| Beaufort Number | Name | Miles Per Hour | Kilometers Per Hour |
|---|---|---|---|
| 0 | Calm | less than 1 | less than 1 |
| 1 | Light air | 1-3 | 1-5 |
| 2 | Light breeze | 4-7 | 6-11 |
| 3 | Gentle breeze | 8-12 | 12-19 |
| 4 | Moderate breeze | 13-18 | 20-28 |
| 5 | Fresh breeze | 19-24 | 29-38 |
| 6 | Strong breeze | 25-31 | 39-49 |
| 7 | Moderate gale | 32-38 | 50-61 |
| 8 | Fresh gale | 39-46 | 62-74 |
| 9 | Strong gale | 47-54 | 75-88 |
| 10 | Whole gale | 55-63 | 89-102 |
| 11 | Storm | 64-73 | 103-118 |
| 12-17 | Hurricane | 74 and above | 119 and above |

**Beaufort Wind Scale**

Did you know that wind is air moving from a high-pressure to a low-pressure area? The greater the difference in pressure, the faster the wind moves. If air pressure differences are slight, you may feel a gentle breeze, but when differences in air pressure are extreme, air may rush to the low pressure area at speeds that can shatter or pick up buildings. The Beaufort wind scale shows how wind speeds are classified and lists the velocities of winds in different types of storms. The most violent winds, those numbered twelve to seventeen, are hurricane force. A hurricane belongs to a category of wind systems called *cyclones*, in which winds circle around low-pressure centers. Most severe storms develop in cyclonic wind systems.

**Effect on Land**

Calm; smoke rises vertically.

Weather vanes inactive; smoke drifts with air.

Weather vanes active; wind felt on face; leaves rustle.

Leaves and small twigs move; light flags extend.

Small branches sway; dust and loose paper blow about.

Small trees sway; waves break on inland bodies of water.

Large branches sway; umbrellas difficult to use.

Whole trees sway; difficult to walk against the wind.

Twigs broken off trees; walking against wind very difficult.

Slight damage to buildings; shingles blown off roofs.

Trees uprooted; considerable damage to buildings.

Widespread damage; very rare occurence.

Violent destruction.

## A Hurricane Forms

Hurricanes begin when warm, humid air rises rapidly. In a hurricane, winds rage around a low-pressure center at speeds of more than 74 miles (120 km) per hour.

In tropical waters, such as the Caribbean Sea or the northern and central Indian Ocean, water warms in the intense, direct rays of the sun. Tropical waters are warmest in late summer and early autumn.

The warmer and the more humid air is, the faster it rises. Therefore, a hurricane depends on both heat and moisture to feed it. The low-pressure area created by ascending warm tropical air is called a tropical depression. Hurricane Georges was born in a tropical depression north of the equator and west of Africa.

As warm air laden with microscopic water droplets rises, cooler air rushes in to replace it. Winds swirl about the center, increasing in velocity and force. As winds accelerate in tropical depressions, they may gather enough strength to erupt into hurricanes.

**Eye of a Hurricane**

In a tropical depression, the rapidly rising air builds a towering cloud. The clouds in hurricanes can dump as much as 20 inches of rain or other precipitation in a few hours.

The low-pressure center, called the *eye*, may be 10 to 50 miles (16 to 80 km) in diameter. Shaped something like a cylinder, the eye extends from the ground to the top of the clouds; within the eye the air is still. When the eye passes over an area, the wind dies, the skies may clear, and weather conditions may become sunny and fair; but when the eye moves on, the storm bears down again with full fury.

When hurricanes pass over land, fierce winds and heavy rainfall pound everything in their path. The savage gusts uproot trees and level buildings. What the wind spares may be washed away or submerged in floods from the pouring rain.

During hurricanes, wind and low atmospheric pressure can draw up waves as high as 40 feet (12 m), and then the winds can drive the waves onto the shore. Sweeping over the land, these waves can wash away entire villages.

In the Northern Hemisphere, hurricanes usually migrate west, then north, then northeast. They do not move far inland, because they sustain themselves by feeding off the warm, moist air rising from the oceans.

Some hurricanes form at sea and then lose their force before ever reaching land. However, these hurricanes can still present fearful dangers for boats at sea. For centuries, ship captains have used what they know about uneven heating, air pressure, wind, and other weather signs to predict these deadly storms and keep track of their progress.

**What's in a Name?**

Within a given year, tropical storms and hurricanes are named in alphabetical order as they occur. At first, all hurricanes were given women's names, but now women's names alternate with men's names.

The famous U.S. Coast Guard ship *Eagle* was battered and nearly sunk by a hurricane in May 1946 on its first voyage as a U.S. Coast Guard ship. At the time, the world's meteorologists did not have the technology they have today for predicting the formation and paths of hurricanes. Even so, the *Eagle's* captain, Commander Gordon P. McGowan, was able to anticipate a hurricane and monitor its progress by measuring air pressure and noticing certain weather signs.

## A Hurricane at Sea

May 30, 1946, was a proud day for the U.S. Coast Guard vessel *Eagle*, a huge, three-masted sailing ship with giant square sails. World War II was over, and the ship had been turned over from a defeated Germany to the U.S. Coast Guard Academy, which would use her to train officers under sail in the traditional way. On May 30, the *Eagle* was ready to make her first run to her new American home. The day dawned bright and clear, with the sea a dead, flat calm. Instead of hoisting the sails and sailing majestically out of the port, the captain, Commander Gordon P. McGowan, had the crew fire up the engines and depart under power. No one onboard foresaw it, but they would encounter plenty of wind before the voyage was over.

For most of the passage across the Atlantic, the *Eagle* knifed through the water, her billowing sails full of steady wind. As she approached Bermuda, she needed her engines to propel her through a stretch of slick, glassy, windless sea. The *Eagle* chugged to Bermuda under power, her wake the only motion on a sea that otherwise looked like a liquid, almost transparent mirror.

After a few days in Bermuda, the *Eagle's* crew prepared to sail for New York, but when the crew set the sails, they hung, flapping about without a breeze to inflate them. The ship rolled back and forth in swells, or long waves, rolling in from the southeast. Later, McGowan would realize that the long swells should have been a warning to him.

McGowan commanded the crew to lower all sails. The *Eagle's* engines again roared to life. As sunset approached, a rippling breeze rose from the southeast. The crew set the sails and settled down for a tranquil night at sea.

A few hours after midnight, the gentle breeze of the evening changed to a gusty, moaning wind, and the *Eagle* began pitching roughly through the dark sea. McGowan bolted out of his quarters and raced toward the deck where he was enveloped by warm, moist, tropical air. The captain picked his way through the sticky darkness to the steering station.

"How long has this been going on?" he asked.

"It just started, Captain," said the officer on watch.

Suddenly McGowan remembered the long, low swell as the ship left Bermuda. Too late, he realized its significance—a long, low swell with no wind to cause it can be one of the first signs of an approaching hurricane!

By dawn, the barometer needle confirmed McGowan's fears with a sudden drop in air pressure. The rapidly building waves, thick rain squalls, and the plummeting barometer left no doubt that a hurricane was imminent. Driven by the mounting wind, the *Eagle* boiled through the water at top speed.

Huge swells began smacking the ship's rudder with such force that it nearly knocked the helmsmen off their feet. Soon eight men strained at the helm instead of the usual two. Scrutinizing the seas, McGowan told the men to steer the ship one way, then another, trying to keep her running away from the storm while avoiding the biggest of the waves rolling down upon her.

When the wind was roaring along at more than 50 knots, the captain noticed a startling change in the sea. Before, the wind had whipped up whitecaps of foam, but now the blasts of wind sliced off whole wave tops and heaved them through the air as explosions of spray. Soon the wind wailed and screamed at 75 miles per hour or more, and the ship began to pitch and roll in the murderous sea. The storm pelted the ship and its crew with sheets of rain.

Still the barometer fell. When the shrieking of the wind drowned out his commands, McGowan began using hand signals to direct the helmsmen. The upper and lower sails suddenly blew out, leaving only ribbons of sailcloth snapping in the wind.

With his sails shredding, McGowan realized he had no choice—he ordered the helmsmen to heave to, or turn the ship to run wherever the wind took her. As the ship swung on her new course, a huge wave towered over her, collided with the deck—and then was gone. The *Eagle* now ran with the wind. The helmsmen tied the wheel into place and ran to help the rest of the crew.

The ship tore along through the water at 16 knots, faster than she had ever moved before. Soon the brutal wind shredded two more sails, leaving only two sails on the mainmast.

Before long, the ship's anemometer, which measured wind velocity, was pegged at 80 knots, the top of its scale. McGowan craned his neck upward to watch the swells that formed menacing walls of water. As they

*Hurricanes have sunk many ships at sea.*

approached from astern, they towered over the ship.

Each time a monstrous wave reached the *Eagle*, the ship's stern lifted sharply on the face of the wave, tipping the bow downward. The bowsprit knifed into the water, followed by part of the bow. When the stern rode down the back of the wave, the bowsprit burst from the water. A gigantic wave swept under the stern, lifting it high in the air. The *Eagle* slipped down the face of the wave, almost like a surfboard, and, with a deafening bang, drove her bow deep into the solid, green water. With the entire front end of the ship submerged to the base of the foremast, the mainsail billowed out like a balloon, then exploded.

***U.S. Coast Guard Eagle***

When the ship rolled nearly all the way over on its side, McGowan found himself looking almost straight down into the churning sea. Valiantly, the *Eagle* struggled upright. As the crew turned the ship into position, a wave bore down on them like a towering cliff, seeming to rise higher than the masts. To the crew's immense relief, the ship was lifted gently over the crest. McGowan noticed that the barometer was finally holding steady. The pressure was still low, and the storm raging around them was still a ferocious hurricane, but at least the captain and the crew knew that this would be the worst of it.

Before long, the wind speed began to dwindle, and by sunset the storm was over. Back on course, the *Eagle* reached New York the next day, battered by the storm, her new sails in tatters. She wore her wounds proudly, though. Tested by the menacing sea, the *Eagle* had proved herself a seaworthy vessel. To this day she is used to train officers.

**Hurricane Prediction, Warnings, and Preparation**

Today, boat and ship captains need not be taken by surprise. During the mid-1950s, about ten years after the *Eagle's* voyage, meteorologists and weather forecasters developed a coordinated system for tracking hurricanes, and they have continued to make improvements over the years.

Radar and recording devices at sea now feed data to the National Hurricane Center in Florida and the National Oceanic and Atmospheric Administration. Since 1966, weather satellites have been in use, so the National Hurricane Center can follow each storm from its very beginning. Daring pilots, called *hurricane hunters*, fly airplanes into the hurricane itself to gather more information.

Although the exact paths of hurricanes are difficult to predict, most people get advance warning. If you ever receive warning that a hurricane may strike your area, follow the advice of the authorities. Sometimes they may tell you to leave an area before the storm approaches land. If you are not advised to leave the area, authorities will tell you what precautions to take and preparations to make to protect your life and property.

Never underestimate the power of these violent storms. With knowledge and technology, humans can anticipate hurricanes and get out of their way.

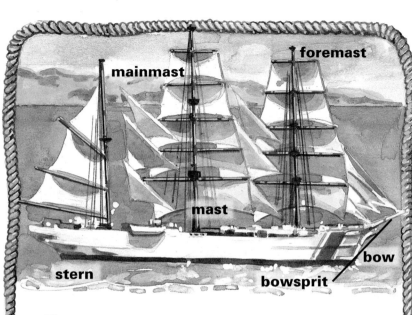

**Glossary**

**astern:** behind a boat

**bow:** the front of a boat

**bowsprit:** a thick pole extending from the bow of
a boat

**foremast:** the mast on a sailing ship closest to the
front

**mainmast:** on a ship with three or more masts, the
second mast back

**stern:** the back of a boat